Items you need when going on an adventure

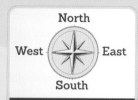

Compass

Ireland Map

Telescope

Magic Whistle

This book belongs to:

About Captain Cillian™

Ahoy readers! Thank you for buying my learning adventure book.

My name is Captain Cillian and I am a fun friendly sailor from Ireland. I love exploring many ports and sailing the seas and oceans.

My learning adventure books and games will take you on a journey of discovery around Ireland and the world! On each adventure, we will encounter many challenges and gain rewards. You will **Explore Ireland, Discover Ocean Facts, Learn Irish words and sounds (see page 20)** plus at the end of each story there is a workbook of activities in the **Create & Play** section.

I'm light, I'm easy to carry and I'm the perfect travel companion for mini explorers!

Captain Cillian™

Wild Atlantic Way

A coastal adventure trail on the west coast of Ireland. It is 2,500km long! It passes through 9 counties in Ireland. The most southern coastal point is called Mizen Head and the most northern coastal point is called Malin Head.

On a lovely sunny Irish spring morning, **Captain** Cillian set sail from **beautiful Dingle** in **County Kerry** in the south-west of Ireland. Today his adventure will take him north along the **Wild Atlantic Way**.

Galway

Dingle

English Words	Focail Ghaeilge
Captain	Captaen
Beautiful	Álainn

Dingle
Dingle is a beautiful town in County Kerry. The coastline includes amazing steep sea-cliffs and sandy beaches.

3

The journey began with blue skies and seagulls flying by to say hello.

"Ahoy, Gully Buddies, top of the morning to you!" smiled Captain Cillian.

OCEAN FACTS

Atlantic Ocean
The Atlantic Ocean is the second largest ocean in the world. It covers 20 percent of the Earth's surface!

Captain Cillian had breakfast on the ship's deck with some warm hot chocolate and thick crusty **bread** with butter… "yum delicious," smiled Captain Cillian.

"Ahoy… Gully Buddies, do you fancy some morning snacks?" asked Captain Cillian. The Gully Buddies swooped down to the ship's deck, "**thank you** Captain Cillian".

English Words	Focail Ghaeilge
Blue sky	Spéir ghorm
Seagulls	Faoileáin
Friend / Buddy	Cara
Bread	Arán
Thank you	Go raibh maith agat

LEARN IRISH

Later on in the morning Captain Cillian
went **fishing** for his **lunch**. He set up
his fishing rod with some **bait**.

"A juicy worm will do the trick!"
laughed Captain Cillian.

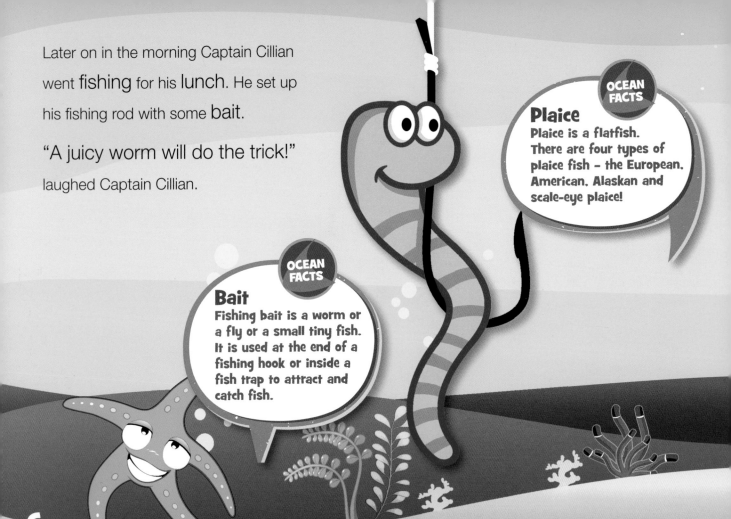

OCEAN FACTS

Plaice
Plaice is a flatfish.
There are four types of
plaice fish – the European,
American, Alaskan and
scale-eye plaice!

OCEAN FACTS

Bait
Fishing bait is a worm or
a fly or a small tiny fish.
It is used at the end of a
fishing hook or inside a
fish trap to attract and
catch fish.

"Bingo! I got it,"

shouted Captain Cillian. "A fine catch, **plaice fish**. This will make a lovely lunch that will give me lots of **energy** for my ocean adventure **today**."

LEARN IRISH

English Words	Focail Ghaeilge
Fishing	Iascaireacht
Lunch	Lón
Energy	Fuinneamh
Today	Inniu

Their journey continued. In the **afternoon** the **wind** became very strong and grey **clouds** gathered over the ship.

Shipmate Freddy Monkey roared "Captain Cillian! There is a storm ahead, we'd better get ready. Pull down the sails, take the wheel and steer us to shore safely."

The storm raged on as Captain Cillian and the crew struggled to keep the ship steady.

Captain Cillian was **nervous.** He knew they needed to sail away from the storm and reach land quickly. "Check our **navigation** maps, Polly Parrot, what options do we have?" asked Captain Cillian.

OCEAN FACTS

Navigation

Navigating ships at sea involves checking the maps and controlling the movement of a ship from one place to another.

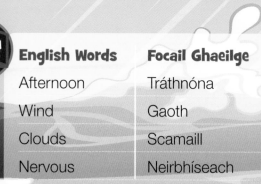

LEARN IRISH

English Words	Focail Ghaeilge
Afternoon	Tráthnóna
Wind	Gaoth
Clouds	Scamaill
Nervous	Neirbhíseach

The rain was crashing down on the ship and the sea began to swell. Then suddenly, a large **wave** pushed the ship five metres high in the air! "Hold on tight Polly Parrot and I'll straighten this out!" roared Captain Cillian. "We need our buddy **Dolphin** Rian to direct us safely to a port, away from this **stormy sea**."

Captain Cillian blew into his magical ocean wind **whistle** three times. Then suddenly, out of the sea jumped Dolphin Rian.

OCEAN FACTS

Dolphins

Dolphins are related to whales. They are powerful swimmers and are extremely playful and active. They can leap as high as 7 metres in the air! Dolphins have a language of their own in the form of whistling sounds.

English Words	Focail Ghaeilge
Wave	Tonn
Dolphin	Deilf
Stormy sea	Farraige stoirmiúil
Whistle	Feadóg

LEARN IRISH

"Hey, Captain Cillian, what brings you out on this stormy sea?" said Dolphin Rian. "We need to get you and Polly Parrot to shore safely, follow me and we will head into shore on the Gulf Stream."

Gulf Stream

The Gulf Stream is a powerful, warm Atlantic ocean current. It starts in Florida in America and follows the eastern coastline of the United States and Newfoundland. It then crosses the Atlantic Ocean over to Ireland.

English Words	Focail Ghaeilge
The shore	An cladach
A plan	Plean
Follow me	Lean mé

Dolphin Rian emerged from the sea once again and shouted "Okay Captain Cillian, I have a **plan**. Galway Bay is just 20 miles north east. **Follow me** through the **waves** and we should reach Galway city harbour before it gets dark."

Waves

OCEAN FACTS

Oceans are always moving. The tides, currents and waves move the oceans. Waves are created by winds blowing over the surface of the oceans. The stronger the winds, the larger the waves.

Polly Parrot shouted from the lookout tower "Ahoy Captain Cillian, land ahead, Galway Bay, what a beauty!"

Dolphin Rian swam ahead to alert the Harbourmaster that Captain Cillian and his ship need permission and assistance to dock in Galway harbour.

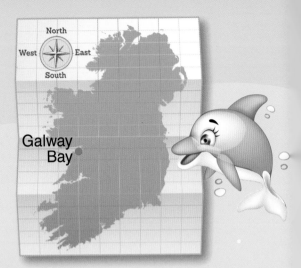

Galway Bay

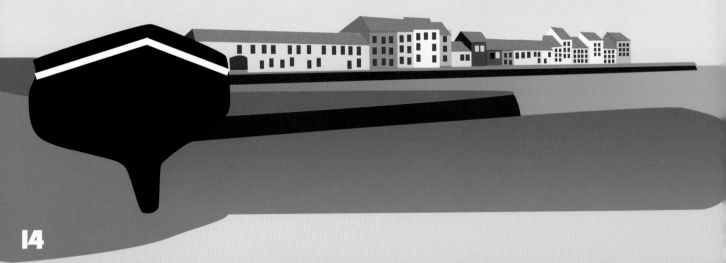

English Words	Focail Ghaeilge
Land	An talamh
Swim	Snámh
The ship	An long

OCEAN FACTS

Harbourmaster

A Harbourmaster is the person responsible for protecting the harbour or port. They ensure the safety of ships and sailing boats landing and docking.

"At last we will be safe", said Captain Cillian. "The Harbourmaster will help us steer the ship into Galway harbour. We need dinner and a deep sleep tonight. We will make a new adventure plan in the morning."

"Thanks Dolphin Rian. What would we do without you and your super sea senses? Until we meet again, best buddy," smiled Captain Cillian.

"Oh I do love the sea and the surprises it brings every day. Good night, sleep tight to all my learning adventure buddies!"

EXPLORE IRELAND

Galway

Galway City is the fourth largest city in Ireland. It is known for its festivals, the Spanish Arch, the Salthill Prom and the Long Walk!

English Words	Focail Ghaeilge
Dinner	Dinnéar
Sleep	Codladh
Adventure	Eachtraíocht
Love	Grá
Good Night	Oíche Mhaith

LEARN IRISH

The End

Irish words and sounds with Captain Cillian

Page	English	Irish	Sounds like
3	Captain	Captaen	Cap-tane
	Beautiful	Álainn	All-in
5	Friend	Cara	Caw-rah
	Blue sky	Spéir ghorm	Spare g-ur-um
	Seagulls	Faoileáin	f-wail-on
	Bread	Arán	Are-on
	Thank you	Go raibh maith agat	g-uh row moh aw-g-ut
7	Fishing	Iascaireacht	Eesk-are-ugh-t
	Lunch	Lón	Loan
	Energy	Fuinneamh	f-win-iv
	Today	Inniu	In-nw-uh
9	Afternoon	Tráthnóna	Tr-aw-no-nah
	Clouds	Scamaill	Sc-om-al
	Wind	Gaoth	g-wee

Page	English	Irish	Sounds like
9	Nervous	Neirbhíseach	Nerve-eesh-ugh
11	Whistle	Feadóg	Fa-d-oh-g
	Stormy sea	Farraige stoirmiúil	Far-ig-ah st-ur-im-ool
	Wave	Tonn	Tonne
	Dolphin	Deilf	Delph
12	The shore	An cladach	Un cl-ad-ugh
	A plan	Plean	plan
	Follow me	Lean mé	Lan may
15	The ship	An long	Un lung
	Swim	Snámh	Sn-aw-v
	Land	An talamh	Un tall-umh
17	Adventure	Eachtraíocht	Aw-k-tree-ugh-t
	Love	Grá	Gr-aw
	Sleep	Codladh	Cul-ah
	Dinner	Dinnéar	Din-air
	Good night	Oíche mhaith	Ee-ha wh-ah

EXPLORE IRELAND   LEARN IRISH   OCEAN FACTS   CREATE & PLAY

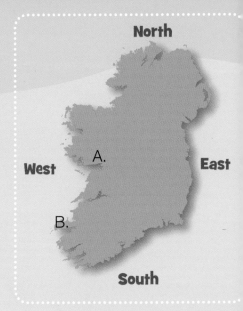

North

West   A.   East

B.

South

1. Write two places on the map of Ireland from this adventure?

A. ....

B. ....

2. Find the words in the puzzle!

BREAD   SEA
DOLPHIN   SHIP
GALWAY   STORM
MAP

K	Y	S	E	A	H	D	V
Z	M	G	O	V	O	E	N
M	Y	A	W	L	A	G	M
D	C	L	P	Q	P	N	R
F	A	H	S	I	G	Q	O
Y	I	E	H	E	A	C	T
N	P	S	R	Q	X	A	S
J	W	U	S	B	H	K	O

4. Name Captain Cillian's friends on this adventure?

....

....

5. Explain how waves are created?

....

....

. List four new Irish words you learned on this adventure?

1. ....

2. ....

3. ....

4. ....

. Visit **www.captaincillian.com** (click on *Create and Play* button) and download free drawings to colour in or create your own adventure story.

Can you spot 5 differences?

Copy this picture - using the grid

Add some colour to your new masterpiece

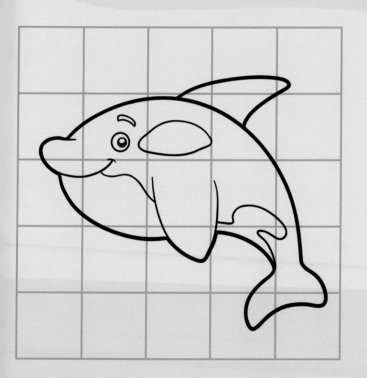

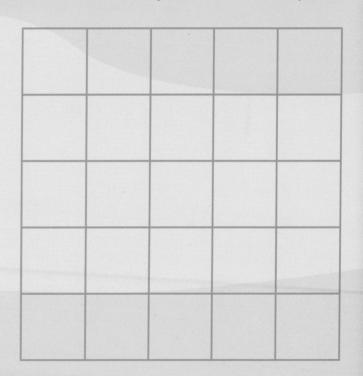

Can you match the correct fish with its shape

26

Our planet is known as "The Blue Planet" because it looks like a blue ball from outer space. This blue colour is because of our oceans!

The world's oceans contain enough water to fill a cube with edges over 1000 kilometres (621 miles) in length!

The largest ocean on Earth is the Pacific Ocean, it covers around 30% of the Earth's surface.

The deepest known area of the Earth's oceans is known as the Mariana Trench. It's deepest point measures 11km.

There are five oceans on Planet Earth - the Pacific Ocean, the Atlantic Ocean, the Indian Ocean, the Arctic Ocean and the Southern Ocean.

Answer, page 24

North

North West

North East

West

East

South West

South East

South

Malin Head

Giant's Causeway

SCHOOL

Donegal

Belfast

Sligo

Westport

SCHOOL

Athlone

Dublin

Galway

SCHOOL

Limerick

SCHOOL

Waterford

Wexford

Dingle

Cork

Mizen Head

Captain Cillian's Favourite Crossword

Down
1. Carries people on water, *clue: we row it!*
3. The leader of a ship
4. A great catch, delicious to eat too
5. The Country where Captain Cillian lives
6. Baddies of the sea
7. Found on the beach

Across
2. Captain Cillians friend Freddy is a ...
3. The edges of land that touch the sea
7. Carries people and goods on the high seas
8. A star shaped fish is called a ...
9. We put this in buckets to make castles.

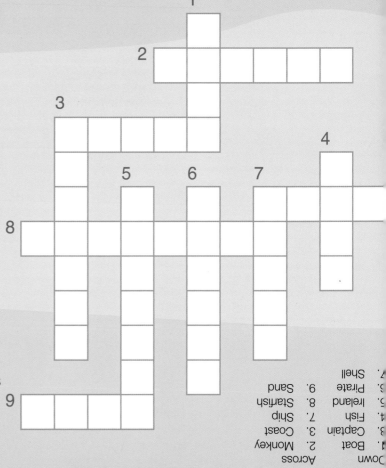

28